The Pretence of Understanding

Beth Davies

NEW**POETS**LIST

the poetry business

Published 2023 by
New Poets List
The Poetry Business
Campo House,
54 Campo Lane,
Sheffield S1 2EG

ISBN 978-1-914914-51-5
eBook ISBN 978-1-914914-52-2
Typeset by Utter
Cover image: Annie Spratt on Unsplash
Printed by Biddles Books

Smith|Doorstop Books are a member of Inpress:
www.inpressbooks.co.uk

Distributed by NBN International, 1 Deltic Avenue,
Rooksley, Milton Keynes MK13 8LD

The Poetry Business gratefully acknowledges
the support of Arts Council England.

Supported by
ARTS COUNCIL
ENGLAND

Contents

In memory of my grandparents, with love

Rat Dissection

She is crucified against cardboard,
stomach cruelly exposed. I'm surprised
how easy it is to cut through skin.

I try not to think about
my own pale flesh. The intricate mess
glistens beneath. *Intestine, lungs,*

liver, kidney, spleen ... Not neatly
arranged like textbook diagrams. The stench
fills me, threatens to empty me out.

Is this how we all eventually smell? I am lucky
not to know the answer. Opened insides
reveal harsh simplicity. The guts

are only a tangle of tubes, the brain
a lump of cells, the heart a bag of muscle.
I cannot find the signs of how

she moved, how she thought,
how she felt. In the end
there is only meat.

Familial Scriptures

In my house, we are a family
of atheists with biblical names.
My father and brother are both
faithless gospels. My name is
the town of Lazarus – a place of miracles,

where things did not stay dead. My mother
hasn't sat through a service in years
yet can't walk past a Catholic church
without entering. She doesn't believe
in God, but her hands still do. I watch

as she crosses herself at the altar:
bowed head, fingertips flying
to the four points her father
taught her. He treasured his faith
like a rusted heirloom.

My grandma, who used to say
it was all nonsense, finds hymns easier
than speech now. I don't know
what the sacred is, but I hear it
in her trembling voice.

The Garden at William Street

The plants have outlawed us from your house
by barricading the garden door. We become
fairytale princes, pushing aside briars,
hacking at what was once well tended.
Mum strains against secateurs: the slow
slice of metal through wood, the release
when a branch falls. I drag thorny limbs
into the forest and cast them among nettles.

Later, at the care home, you don't notice
our scratched legs, dirty shoes, the tang
of grass clippings. Your mind too is overgrown,
your words behind thorns, my name
a house you cannot reach. I hold your hand,
wishing I could tame that wilderness.

All I Know of Ghanaian Rain

Next morning, they told
of the storm-soaked night. I wondered how
I'd slept through, wished I hadn't. Rain –
like home – was something I dreamt

before waking to dust and heat.
Two months later, the second storm
woke me with iron drumbeats,
the fan silenced. How could I resist

reunion? I crept outside to greet the downpour
in flip-flops and pyjamas, my face upturned
to the flashbulb sky, sweat washing from my skin,
every hole in the yard overflowing.

The Wonderful Everyday

What strangers live here? I look around the living room
for clues. Maybe he's the music lover and it's his record player
on the side table, brand new but missing the needle.

She loves to read her favourite book over and over,
but buys a new copy each time (the same edition),
hoping for a different ending. Identical books

crowd the shelves. He doesn't mind because the spines
match the wallpaper. The drawing on the fridge shows
a triangle-roofed house, a row of faceless stick figures

waving in the front garden – parental love evident
from the act of display. I wonder whether they are happy,
wearing their stock smiles in a wedding photo, teeth

impossibly bright. In the kitchen cupboard, I find jars filled
with pictures of food. They sustain themselves
on the ideas of things. Is this enough to build a life from?

Are these three walls enough? Maybe they are saving up
for a fourth. Looking up, I see the ceiling is much further away
than it should be – enough empty air to call *sky*.

Is that where they've gone, the family who lived here?
I imagine following them up the half-made stairs
onto an upper floor that doesn't exist.

Cleaning the Pool

Each day we fished six- and eight-legged
things from the water, the net teeming
with bugs that had met their chlorinated end.

Despite our parents' disapproval,
we tipped the bodies into a glass jar
and kept it by the poolside – a morbid

greenhouse, baking in the Italian sun.
We did not try to identify species.
We had no need for that pretence

of understanding. Our fascination was in the
unsorted tangle of shell and wing and abdomen,
in which it was hard to tell where one

ended and the next began. One kid
speculated how the creatures would look
as they dried out. He asked the adults

to place their bets on which parts
would decay and what would be left
behind. Another declared our aim

to fill the jar to the top. He kept track
of the rising line with the same enthusiasm
he showed over his *Match Attax* album.

A third held that vessel with reverence,
always made sure we placed it
somewhere safe. When I gazed into the jar

like it was a crystal ball, I could almost hear
legs scuttling, wings fluttering, the whisper
of what they'd once been. At the end

of the week, our parents made us
throw away the contents of the jar.
I don't remember if we grieved.

Sometimes I Miss my Housemates' Crockery

I picture us there: one making cups of tea;
another defrosting a lump of bolognese; one perched
on the worktop, spinning a story from her day.

Time doesn't pass in the kitchen,
we'd joke, to justify those hours.
We were meant to be studying

but deadlines couldn't cross
the threshold; the clock stopped
and no one replaced the battery.

If time doesn't pass in the kitchen
at 11 Crossview Terrace, we are all
still there, fending off the future.

Back in the city for graduation,
I walked past the house, hoping
to spot one of us through the window.

Instead, I made eye contact
with a stranger as she got up
from the sofa. Those rooms now hold

her group of housemates: their in-jokes,
their piles of washing-up. She looked away
and walked into the kitchen, out-of-sight.

I strained my ears, unsure
whether I was listening for laughter,
or a newly ticking clock.

Visitation from Past Self

After Bryony Littlefair

Reach by S Club 7 has just come on
and I'm about to take a gulp of vodka-coke
when I notice her on the edge of my vision:
my eight-year-old self, a few steps away, somehow
unjostled by the crowd. She's watching me
and I stop dancing, self-conscious

in a way I don't remember her ever being. I abandon
my drink somewhere and crouch to her level.
I sang this at my Y2 Leavers Assembly! she yells.
Yes, I remember! I shout back. I nearly say
I think of her whenever I hear this song,
but I don't want to seem obsessed with her.

She's too young to be here, so I take her hand
to guide her outside. Instead, she ends up
leading, pulling me through the crowd.
The strobe lights blink her out of existence
and back in. Her hand is small and sweaty.
I grip tightly for fear she'll disappear.

Out on the street, I've no cover
for not knowing what to say to her.
I never got the hang of talking to children,
nor to myself. She asks *What's it like to be old?*
I protest that I'm only twenty-five.
But you are a grown-up, she declares

like she's won an argument. I shrug,
unsure how to respond to this appraisal.
She inspects me again, the boldness
of her gaze absurd on her young face.
Were you really this confident? I ask.
I was sometimes, she says. *Anyway,*

you imagine me like this. Inside,
Reach for the stars is fading
out. We stand together, listening.
As she looks up at me, the lyrics
are a question in her eyes
and I don't know the answer.

Scene

Tonight, they are shouting again
in the gardens behind my house.
The performance drifts over the hedge,
through an open window,

into my kitchen, its voices too distant
for me to follow the plot. I only make out
snatches: a shouted name,
an exclamation of surprise, a scream –

hints of stories unfolding just beyond
the edges of my life. Even without
audible words, the cadence of comedy
is distinct from that of tragedy.

I hear the laughter but not the joke.
Perhaps it is enough that people nearby
are happy. Perhaps I do not need
to know why. When the play ends,

I suppress my instinct
to join in with the applause.

The Road Ran Between Forest and Sea

Getting changed among the trees,
we heard something scuttling in the dark.
When our eyes adjusted, the forest was alive
with crabs, crawling from behind each tree, hidden

in every hollow, camouflaged
so we only saw them when they moved.
They were armoured and pincered,
in contrast to our swimsuit vulnerability.

We ran from the forest and did not return,
preferring to risk exposing ourselves
rather than face the crustacean swarm.
Driving off again, we saw

a crab in the road, remarked
upon it, and swerved round. Another,
and we stopped to let it pass. Soon
there were more. We mourned the first

we failed to avoid. Maybe
we should have realised
what was coming: the road suddenly
paved with crabs, an endless exodus.

It was a long, straight road – no detour
to take, no turn-off to reverse to, no way out
except through. The crabs kept pouring
from the forest. Wincing, we drove on

through the crack and crunch of tyres over shells.
For the rest of the holiday, we were reminded
of our crime by the rental car's fishmonger smell,
splatters on the white paintwork.

Final Visit

We used to read Tennyson
and Wordsworth together. Now

we stick to picture books. Today
it's *Hairy Maclary*. You like

the rhymes and the drawings
of dogs. I start reading to you, but

halfway through the book, you take over
unexpectedly, your voice carried along

by the tide of words, your eyesight
sharp even without your glasses.

When we reach the end, you begin
turning the pages back again.

I can't tell if you've forgotten
the usual direction, or if you

just don't want the story to be over.
You read the whole book in reverse:

animals retreating through hedges,
moonwalking down the street, leaping

backwards over fences, none of them
looking in the direction they are going.

For you, it's no more disjointed
than the other way round.

You don't remember a page
once it's no longer in front of you.

I wonder if we'll stay forever
in this perpetual present, reading

back to front, then front to back, over and over,
trying to make the story return to itself.

A Plea for Future Winters

Don't ever let me say *It's only snow*.
If the season comes when I no longer
watch wide-eyed at windows, when I stop
listening for each footstep crunch and never
run arms-wide into blizzards, if one day,
these Christmas card mornings cannot

make me child again, throw a snowball
in my face. Take me sledging in Bingham Park
on that red toboggan with yellow handles.
Tell me the name of every snowman
I ever built. Remind me how we squealed
when the first flakes fell, how it tasted
to catch wonder on my tongue.

Infestation

The first casualty was a bag of groceries
I found shredded, flour spilling out like entrails.

Every packet bore the marks of small rooting mouths,
no carton left untouched by their irrepressible teeth.

They claimed everything: an act of intimidation,
an assertion of territory, a reminder that this house

does not belong to us. Nor to the landlord, no matter
what the contract says. It belongs to them,

the furry bodies that gather in the damp pit beneath us,
planning to advance upwards. Each night, we hear

knife-scratchings in the walls. They know the ways
of this house. They have watched others like us come

and go. They know the power of the unseen. They know
how easily unsettled we are. My housemate's mum

told her not to leave anything behind in the house
that she was not willing to lose. If they can't find food,

who knows what they'll devour? Our clothes,
our books, the remnants of our third-year sanity?

All our possessions are being eyed up by a rodent
multitude. We sense them under our feet,

above our heads, always just beyond
the edges of our vision. For now, they lie in wait.

Exhumation

Picturing a dark looming shape, I bring everything black
out into the light. Only after digging do I find a bundle,

wrinkled and unremarkable. I inhale, imagine a whiff
of Catholic incense. Instead, it smells like anything

that has festered in a laundry basket for over a year.
I had feared washing it might induce its next duty.

To appear prepared would have been distasteful.
Better to keep it out of sight. Better to forget.

After washing, I'll hang it on my wardrobe door,
where it can't touch what is clean and ordinary.

It will hover there, empty as a ghost.

Floriography

Like me, they were afraid
of how words bloom between
people. They preferred the silence
of a bouquet left on a doorstep or a heart
worn in a buttonhole. They understood

what I don't: the significance
of a carnation's shade, the melancholy
of a red geranium in a left hand,
how orange lilies know as much of hatred
as fists do, the bittersweet of nightshade

and truth. Is there a flower
for the feelings that have taken root
in my chest? If I pressed petals
between these pages, would you know
what I am trying to say?

If You Cut an Earthworm in Half

it becomes two worms. Or so we believed as children.
They wriggle in opposite directions without looking back.

Does this mean each worm contains an infinite number
of worms, all waiting to be cut loose? I once watched

a girl in the playground test this fact. A small crowd gathered
in anticipation. We wouldn't have done it, but we wanted

to see it done. She – perhaps the cruellest of us, perhaps simply
the boldest – applied the edge of her heel with brutal precision.

We observed the two halves intently, but neither moved.
This was disappointing. We wanted evidence that a severing

can bring freedom. We wanted proof that being segmented is a strength.
We wanted to believe that anything is survivable. But the worm

– or worms – lay still. They shone pink against the grey tarmac.
We left them there. Even so, I like to think that, after we dispersed,

the two worms twitched, stretched,

and went their separate ways.

Perhaps The Careers Advisor Would Have Said

When cleaning your student kitchen, search for omens in stubborn stains.
Each smudge is shaped like something, even if you cannot tell what.

Pause your scrubbing to gaze into the oven door.
It lacks the charm of a crystal ball, but it's worth a try.

If the paint peels when you take down your posters,
trace the cracks. One might be a heart line, another a life.

Make tea for your parents. Regret the limited mystical powers
of PG Tips. Examine the bottom of their mugs anyway.

Back in your childhood bedroom, gut your suitcase like an ancient
sacrifice. Watch the dirty laundry fall. Inspect the entrails.

Check your university email. The unread messages
are like magpies: *one for sorrow, two for mirth.*

If – as is probably the case – their numbers stretch far
beyond the end of the rhyme, write some new verses.

Lay your old lecture notes out like tarot, and hope
they'll finally tell you something.

The Doll

After the rituals of washing and dressing her
begin to lose their charm, my interest shifts
towards examining her anatomy.

I run my fingers over the furrows in her scalp –
a ploughed plastic field to mimic hair. I inspect
her knuckles, compare the intricate details

to the creases in my own skin, imagine
each indentation carefully carved
by a master craftsman.

I knock on her torso and listen
to the hollow echo. Her head is the most tender
part of her. I push the scalp inwards,

forming a deep crater. It rises resiliently
back into shape. When I press both sides
at once, she exhales, as if sighing

or preparing to speak. At night, I place my torch
against her skull, so the emptiness inside her fills
with light. It shines out from every inch

of her small hard body. She glows red,
transformed into a strange devilish thing.
I relish that power. Or I envy it.

At the Wake, We Talked About Fish

She used to get them delivered. She liked
to sleep in, so the fishmonger would post them
through the letterbox. I imagined a mackerel
in a stamped addressed envelope, the paper wet
with oil, juices leaking onto the floorboards. Or else,
a freshly caught trout, landing on the doormat
as onto the deck of a ship, still alive,
still gasping, still choking and shuddering

before stillness. The delivery was cancelled
years ago. Even so, we all thought about a fish lying
for too long in the hallway, no one coming
to put it in the freezer, the smell
filling that old house as it rotted, the stench
nearly as horrible as what it meant.

Carolling

My childhood blurs in yellow light
and cinnamon air, the year
irrelevant. A single *Gloria* holds
all my Christmas Eves: nights

when we breathed dragon-smoke,
clutched rain-crinkled paper and sang
to our streets, two tunes at once and all
out of time. It's the closest I've come

to faith. Out-of-tune voices made
the lyrics feel true, made me wonder
if the streetlamp was a star,
guiding us somewhere.

I Often Dream of Ladders

Last night, I emerged into a long room.
Two rows of cots lined the walls, a baby in each one.
I somehow knew each baby would grow
into someone from my life. Here, red-faced
and wailing, was the boy I sat next to in Y10 English.

Sucking her thumb, the girl at whose house party
I first tried beer. And waving his tiny fists,
a university coursemate who always had something
to say in seminars. In every crib, another acquaintance
who was born the same year as me.

As I peered down at an infant who would one day
be my flatmate, a deep urge seized hold of me –
not broodiness, but the need to find the baby
who would become me. I walked the middle
of the two rows, looking left then right

at each pair of cots, as if carefully crossing
a very wide road. I thought I'd recognise
myself, as a mother recognises her child,
but I searched without success. Even so,
I could not rid myself of the longing

to hold that tiny wide-eyed creature, the part of me
around which the rest grew. What else is the point
of time travel, if not to cradle the smallest, softest
versions of ourselves, if not to sing a lullaby,
to try and soothe them when they cry?

Acknowledgements

This pamphlet - like so many of the good things in my life - would not have been possible without the love and support of my family. My parents in particular deserve a mention here for their steadfast belief in me and my creative endeavours. Thank you for being there for me through my stress and joy and doubt. It means the world.

If not for the creative communities I've been part of over the years, I'd be a much worse poet – in fact, I'm not sure that I'd even feel able to call myself a poet at all.

I'm grateful to Hive South Yorkshire, an organisation which has had an enormously positive impact on my writing journey since I attended my first meeting of Sheffield Young Writers over eight years ago. I'm particularly indebted to Vicky Morris for her continual support of my writing, including helping me prepare my winning New Poets entry.

I'm also grateful to The Writing Squad, for the innumerable opportunities and experiences they have given me. I particularly want to mention Steve Dearden, who makes things happen, and Stevie Ronnie, who provided invaluable feedback on many of these poems.

And I'm grateful to Durham University Poetry Society and Slam Team for providing a poetic community that challenged and inspired me. Shout out to Kym Deyn and Jay Hulme, a terrific set of 'poetry parents'.

I'm grateful to everyone in each of the communities mentioned above, for making me feel like I'm part of something wonderful.

Thank you to The Poetry Business and to Anthony Anaxagorou for believing in these poems, and to Suzannah Evans for her excellent editorial advice. Thank you also to the following journals, anthologies, and websites for publishing versions of some of these poems: *Atrium*, *Dear Life* (Hive South Yorkshire), *Poetry Wales*, *Pulp Poets Press*, *Surfing the Twilight* (Hive South Yorkshire), *Ten Poems about Flowers* (Candlestick Press), *The Gentian*, and *The Poetry Society*.

Finally, thank you to my friends: the ones I'm lucky enough to still have in my life from school; the ones I was lucky enough to find at Durham (some of whom get a cameo on page 14); and the ones I've been lucky enough to meet since then (some of whom witnessed me absolutely freaking out when I found out I'd won the New Poets Prize). Your friendships have enriched my life in ways that I don't know how to fully express, even with poetry on my side.